HOW THE BIBLE WAS BUILT

How the Bible Was Built

Charles Merrill Smith

James W. Bennett

WILLIAM B. EERDMANS PUBLISHING COMPANY

GRAND RAPIDS, MICHIGAN / CAMBRIDGE, U.K.

Wm. B. Eerdmans Publishing Co.
255 Jefferson Ave. S.E., Grand Rapids, Michigan 49503 /
P.O. Box 163, Cambridge CB3 9PU U.K.

Printed in the United States of America

10 09 08 07 06   7 6 5 4

ISBN-10: 0-8028-2943-0
ISBN-13: 978-0-0828-2943-6

www.eerdmans.com

Contents

Contents

Contents

Contents

Preface

A Labor of Love

This wonderful book comes with a story. It is, literally, the manuscript found in the basement, some years after the author's death.

Its author, Charles Merrill Smith, penned a number of provocative books of religious commentary during his life, which ended in February of 1985. He wrote the runaway bestseller *How to Become a Bishop Without Being Religious,* which was published by Doubleday in 1965. His other religious books include *When the Saints Go Marching Out* (Doubleday, 1969) and *The Case of a Middle Class Christian* (Word, 1973).

Later in his writing career, Mr. Smith turned to fiction, writing the novels which make up the *Reverend Randollph* mystery series.

How the Bible Was Built was discovered by his widow, Betty, in February of 1999 as she was sorting through some of his papers and notebooks. She found, however, not *a* manuscript, but several. It was evident from the several drafts and revisions that Mr. Smith had worked on the book over a lengthy period of time, and pursued it from two or three different angles. Most of this writing was done, most likely, between 1980 and the time of his death.

Betty asked me if I would be willing to undertake the chore of "shaping this stuff up" so that it would be suitable for publication. I was happy to have a go at it, not only because of the book's substantial merit, but because of my long and gratifying relationship with its author.

Charles Merrill Smith was a mentor and second father to me for nearly thirty years. He encouraged me to think, and to write. Such success as I have had as an author is in large part owing to his support, encouragement, and taskmastering.

Most of the books I have written are fiction, for young adults as well as adults. The only book to my credit which is "religious" is *A Quiet Desperation,* an autobiographical faith journey published in 1983 by Thomas Nelson. Charles Merrill Smith wrote the preface for that book; here I try to return the favor.

Truth be told, though, a labor of love is still *labor.* Parts of Mr. Smith's manuscript were relatively polished, while others were not so completely developed. Although his first draft of the book indicates a teenage audience, his notes make it plain that revisions were aimed at expanding its readership.

While trying to maintain the integrity of the book each step of the way, there were still revisions I had to make. His knowledge of the Bible, for instance, far surpassed his understanding of architectural particulars.

Some of the necessary steps were editorial ones, others involved cobbling together portions of different drafts, and still others amounted to little more than copyediting.

I took the liberty, from time to time, of doing what my editors always do for me: polishing the prose, varying the sentence structure, sharpening the syntax, and the like. Charles was a perfectionist; all of these things he would have done himself, had he lived just a little longer.

In all cases I made it my central goal to keep the essential Charles Merrill Smith alive throughout the book — his prose, his way, his soul. I hope I have succeeded in that effort.

As you will see in Chapter One, Mr. Smith's first inspiration to undertake this book was triggered by questions from his granddaughter, Julia. With that in mind, I think we are on safe ground in dedicating *How the Bible was Built* to her.

For Julia, then.

JAMES W. BENNETT

Chapter One

How This Book Was Built

The Bible, always the world's bestseller, is setting new sales records every year. Its popularity has never been greater. It is available in many translations and paraphrases — all of them in wide use.

Yet most Bible readers would find it difficult to answer such questions as: How did the Bible get to be the Bible? What kind of literature is in it? Who wrote it? Why were the various books written? Why were they chosen to be included in the Bible? When were they written? Why do we have four books on the life of Jesus in the New Testament instead of just one? What is the Apocrypha?

This book answers just such questions. It tells the story of the writing of the Bible step by step. It is a book of facts. No particular perspective about the Bible is presented or urged on the reader. Those who hold conservative views of the scriptures can pick it up without fear that the book will undermine their faith.

Those of a more liberal persuasion can do the same.

Those who hold no strong religious convictions of any kind, but believe the Bible to be an essential part of our culture will find it just as useful.

Benefits of Reading This Book

What started out as a book for teenagers and young adults has become, with each successive draft (or revision), a book targeted at a much wider readership. Not just teenagers, but parents, teachers, spiritual seekers, even ordinary churchgoers curious about the Bible will find much to learn in it.

I have said that Christians of various backgrounds and predispositions will benefit from this book, and enjoy it as well. After all, facts are facts. Bible scholars, for example, are conservative and liberal, Roman Catholic and Protestant and Jewish, and can differ widely on how they interpret the Bible. But they are in general agreement with regard to the fundamental facts about the Bible.

Is it important to know these facts? Yes indeed. Some readers might wonder, *why can't I just enjoy reading the*

Bible without going into all these facts? The answer would be that of course they can, because that is precisely what many people do. It is the belief here, however, that reading the Bible will mean more to people if they know what they are reading.

People are reading the Bible in record numbers today. They are taking it seriously. But if they are to be "at home" with the Bible instead of treating it as a remote and mysterious document, then knowing these facts will be beneficial to them.

To enable people to know exactly what the Bible is; to make it possible for them to read it with real comprehension; to make it clear to them where the Bible came from, and why these special books came to be collected as holy scripture — these are the purposes of this book.

Most books written about the Bible mix facts with doctrinal or theological perspectives. This is necessary and legitimate for books meant for use as evangelical tools or as instruments for sectarian instruction. But if there is a book which sets forth briefly and clearly the story behind the Bible, sets it forth unadorned by theological or sectarian persuasion, I am not aware of it. That is what this book seeks to be.

The Inspiration According to Julia

Originally, the book was inspired by my fourteen-year-old granddaughter Julia. One day she began asking me questions about the Bible, asking them with almost machine-gun rapidity. *Where did the Bible come from? Who wrote it? Who said it was the Bible?* And on and on.

When I reported the conversation to Julia's mother, she said she wished I would find a book which would tell the story of the Bible that all the grandchildren could read. They were growing up rather ignorant of the Bible, she declared, and she didn't like that. As a matter of fact, she said, she didn't know as much about the Bible as she would like to know. She'd welcome a simple, understandable, factual story of the Bible herself.

Since I couldn't find such a book, I decided to write one.

I am not a Bible scholar. I am a seminary-trained, ordained clergyman who has spent more than three decades in the parish ministry. The Bible, of course, has always been my basic working tool. If there is a fact about the Bible I don't know — and there are many — I know where to find it. I rely on the works of scholars whose credentials and integrity are well established.

Like every person of faith, I have an attitude toward the Bible. But I have not permitted it to intrude in this

4

book. This is a book of information, not evangelism. If the Bible plays any part at all in our lives — as a guide for living, a handbook of devotion, or a source for understanding our culture — it is important that all of us, young and old, have this information.

Chapter Two

How the Bible Was Built

When members of a family build a house, they first talk about it. Maybe the conversation goes on for a long time. Someone thinks of an idea for the house. Someone else makes a suggestion. The house gradually takes shape — but only in the mind of the family.

There are many things to consider over time — where will the property be? Who will be the architect? What are the building materials of choice? What about financing the construction?

There comes a day, though, when the actual foundation is laid, and walls go up, and a roof goes on. This may be only the first unit of the house, however. As the years go by, rooms such as a den or library may be added. The house will be made larger. An entire wing may be built, if the need arises.

In other words, the building process can go on for

many years. But the time will come eventually when the family says, *That's all. This house is finished. Nothing more will be added.*

This pretty much describes how the Bible was put together.

It began with people talking about their God, the heroes of their history, and the stories, customs, and beliefs that bound them together as a family of faith.

Then, various members of the family decided to write down these things.

What the Word *Bible* Means

In the early days of Christianity, if you owned a complete Bible, it was inscribed on a number of scrolls. The next time you're at a party or other social setting, you might ask people, "What does the word *bible* mean?" Hardly any of them will know that it comes from the Greek word *biblion,* which means "papyrus scroll." It is a good idea for us to remember this, because it will help us to think of the Bible as made up of many separate scrolls, even though we have it bound up in one book.

There is a unity to the Bible, just as there is a unity to a well-designed house. But the rooms differ in size, purpose, and perspective. If we think of the books of the Bible as rooms in a house, it will help us understand how books as widely different as Psalms and Paul's Letter to the Romans both serve the main purpose of the Bible.

Strange Ideas about the Bible

People, though they may be devout, often have strange ideas about how the Bible came to be.

A friend of mine told me recently of a conversation he had with a man noted for his piety and faithfulness to the church. "I live by the Bible," the man told my friend. "I mean the true Bible, of course. The Bible that King James wrote."

"But," my friend protested, "King James didn't write the Bible."

"Oh yes he did," the man insisted. "It says so right on the flyleaf. They call it the King James Bible, don't they? However," he was willing to add, "King James may have hired some assistants to help him."

And, recently, while listening to a radio interviewer ask people how they liked the New International Version of the Bible, I heard a zealous young Christian answer that she was going to stick with the King James Version because it was the Bible that Jesus wrote.

These people are no doubt sincere. But it subtracts

nothing from our religious sincerity if we recognize the history of how the Bible was created. So let's continue to think of the process of the creation of the Bible along the lines of our house-building analogy.

A House with Two Wings and a Connecting Passage

The house of the Bible has two main wings. The older wing most of us call the Old Testament. The newer wing we call the New Testament. There is a small section of the house, a passageway connecting the two wings, which not everyone uses. It is called the Apocrypha.

The older wing and the Apocrypha were built by a family of faith called the Jews. A family of faith called the Christians came to share this house and added another wing to it — the New Testament.

It took well over a thousand years to construct this house we call the Bible. It took longer than that before it was decided that the house was finished, and that no more rooms should be added.

This, then, is the story of how the Bible was built.

Chapter Three

The First Wing —
the Old Testament

The first part of our house of the Bible is most often referred to as the Old Testament. The family of faith called the Jews came to the land we know as Palestine about 1800 years before the birth of Jesus. They developed a sense of their own identity as a people around the worship of the God *Yahweh*.

They told stories about their people, their leaders, their heroes, and their history. Some of the Jews took it upon themselves to write down these stories and history. Thus, a written record was accumulated.

The Cornerstone of the Bible

The cornerstone of the house of the Bible wasn't laid in place, though, until the seventh century B.C. — fairly well along in Jewish history. There is a fascinating story about how this came about.

The Jewish people had come to be divided into two nations. The northern nation, or kingdom, was called Israel. The southern kingdom was called Judah.

Judah had been ruled for more than fifty years by a king named Manasseh. From the point of view of Jewish religion — the religion of Yahweh — he was an unacceptable king. He promoted the worship of many different gods, and during his reign, every community or village had its own gods to worship. The worship of Yahweh alone pretty much faded away.

Some time after Manasseh died, a king named Josiah came to the throne. He believed in Yahweh and wanted to restore the worship of Yahweh in the kingdom of Judah.

So King Josiah began a program of religious reform. One of his first steps was to repair and rebuild the great Temple in Jerusalem. During the reconstruction, a priest of the Temple discovered, hidden away in some dark nook or cranny, the book that we now call Deuteronomy.

It was written, as best we know, by someone — an unknown prophet, perhaps, or a priest or sage — who lived during the reign of King Manasseh. This person would have had to do his work in secret, hiding the completed book in the Temple in the hope that it would be discovered when brighter days came to the land. The Old Testament records the story of its discovery in 2 Kings, chapters 22 and 23.

King Josiah welcomed the newly-discovered book and made it the program for his reformation. It became the law of the land. Judah was a theocracy, that is to say, a country in which the civil law and the religious law were one and the same. By making this religious writing the law of the land, Josiah gave it special status in the eyes of the people. And when you give a religious writing special status, you have taken the first step toward the creation of a holy scripture.

What Was So Special about the Book of Deuteronomy?

No writing will long continue to be held in high esteem by the people — even if a king says they must respect it — unless they find it worthy, helpful, and meritorious in its own right.

Deuteronomy appealed to the people because it contained the two great elements in the religion of Yahweh — the priestly element and the prophetic element.

When people have strong religious convictions, they put these beliefs and attitudes into rituals and ceremonies. By participating in these ceremonies they dramatize and affirm their beliefs. And these rituals help keep the religion alive. If, for example, Christians didn't have the Sunday church service, or the Mass, or something like them, the faith would soon atrophy, most likely, or die out altogether. The religion of the Jews had its ceremonies and rituals, and these, too, are described in the book of Deuteronomy. This is the *priestly* element.

The religion of the Jews had a concern for how people should behave themselves. It had well-defined ideas about how individuals should treat one another, what is just and right, what God demands of us day in and day out. This is the moral or ethical aspect of religious faith. How God expected the people to behave is the *prophetic* element of Israel's religion described in the book of Deuteronomy.

We could say, then, that Deuteronomy taught the followers of Yahweh how to be reverent and how to be good. That's why the people found it so useful. That's why it became the cornerstone of the Old Testament. Deuteronomy is not the oldest piece of writing in the Old Testament, but it was the first to be looked on as holy scripture.

What Is the Pentateuch?

But it takes more than a cornerstone to form a foundation. In the two hundred years following the discovery of the book of Deuteronomy, several other books were written which were recognized by the people as of great importance to their faith and life. We know these books as Genesis, Exodus, Leviticus, and Numbers. You recognize them as the first four books in the Old Testament as we have it today.

Added to Deuteronomy, these four books complete the section of the Old Testament which we call *the Law*. These five books, taken together, are also called *the Torah* or *the Pentateuch*. And it was the Pentateuch which became holy scripture for the Jewish people. Returning to our metaphor, the Law is the foundation for the Old Testament wing of the house of the Bible.

The Story of the Samaritans

But what about the other 34 books of our Old Testament? Didn't the Jews believe they were sacred writings too?

Well, yes and no. Some did, and others didn't.

About the time the Pentateuch was completed and recognized as holy scripture, the son of a Jewish high priest and a priest himself married a foreign girl. The Jews said this was against the law, so he'd have to send her home. But he said he loved her and wouldn't send her home. This young priest's father-in-law was wealthy, so he built his son-in-law a temple of his own. Thus, the young priest took his family and followers and established his own Jewish religious sect.

This sect recognized the Pentateuch as holy scripture because at this point in Jewish history the five books which comprised it were the only religious writings accepted as sacred. As other books came to be accepted as part of the scripture by most of the Jewish people, this young priest and those of his sect who lived after him continued to believe that only the Law or Pentateuch was sacred.

This sect still survives today. It still accepts only the first five books of the Old Testament as scripture. We know these people as the *Samaritans.* The name was made famous, of course, by Jesus' parable about a good Samaritan.

Another group, called the Sadducees, similarly recognized only the Law as holy scripture. The Sadducees were the royal priests of the religion of Israel. They were the keepers and officials of the Great Temple in Jerusalem. We read about some of their interactions with Jesus in the New Testament. There weren't very many of them, but because of their high position in Jewish life, they were influential.

The vast majority of the Jewish people, however, came to look on the Law as the foundation of their scripture. We can think of the rest of the Old Testament as the roof and walls constructed on this foundation.

The Prophets — the Walls of the House

I hate, I despise your festivals,
    and I take no delight in your solemn
        assemblies . . .
Take away from me the noise of your songs;
    I will not listen to the melody of your harps.
But let justice roll down like waters,
    and righteousness like an ever-flowing stream.

Many readers will find these words familiar, even if they can't say exactly where they are located in the Bible. They come from the fifth chapter of the book of Amos.

Amos was the first of a group of writers whose books comprise part of the Old Testament. We call them *the Literary Prophets.* Amos did his writing in the eighth century — probably about 750 B.C.

Hosea, Micah, and Isaiah wrote at about this same

time. The great literary prophet of the seventh century was Jeremiah. His contemporaries were Nahum, Zephaniah, and Habakkuk. Most of us would think Ezekiel the most important prophet of the sixth century. But this was also the time of Haggai and Zechariah. The fifth-century prophets were Malachi, Obadiah, and Joel.

These individuals wrote a special kind of literature. Though their messages differ in many ways, they claimed to speak for God. Like Amos in the example above, they were very intense and powerful in their style of expression. And they were poets — some of them very good ones. Most of their prophecies were composed in poetic form. Passages from Amos, Isaiah, Jeremiah, and others of these literary prophets have become part of our language and culture today.

The Message of the Prophets

These poets talked about such things as the righteousness of God. That is the main theme in the book of Amos. God, Amos told the people, was righteous, and God expected them to be just and upright and merciful and decent in their living together.

Furthermore, Amos said, God expects this kind of behavior not just of the Jews, but of all people everywhere.

We need to remember that during this period of history, each nation had its own god or gods, and many of the people of Israel thought of Yahweh as Israel's god exclusively. But the prophet Amos said, "No, God is the God of all people. And the most important thing about God is God's righteousness."

This marked a great step forward in religious thought. We call Amos' idea of God *ethical monotheism* — meaning he believed that there is only one God, who demands certain kinds of behavior from all people. We don't know that this idea originated with Amos. But no one before him had ever stated it in such powerful and memorable language.

The prophet-poet Hosea wrote his book not long after Amos. Hosea added something to Amos' idea of God's righteousness. He stressed the redemptive love of God.

In the book of Isaiah, also written around this time, we find beautiful descriptions of the ideal king who will bring in a new age of justice and righteousness. Chapters 40 through 55 of this book talk about how God shapes human history. Also, it is in these chapters that we find the sublime poetry about what scholars call the *suffering servant,* which Christians have traditionally associated with Jesus.

So, on the foundation of the Law, the Jews erected the walls of the house of the Bible and called them *the Prophets.*

Former Prophets and Latter Prophets

But the part of the Old Testament they called the Prophets includes much more than the great literary prophets. The Jews divided this section of the Old Testament into *the Former Prophets* and *the Latter Prophets.* Books such as Samuel and Kings, which we would call books of history, they called prophetic. These books, they said, had a religious purpose and could rightly be grouped under the heading of prophecy.

The list of Former Prophets includes the books of Joshua, Judges, Samuel, and Kings.

The list of Latter Prophets includes Isaiah, Jeremiah, and Ezekiel, plus these twelve shorter prophetic books: Hosea, Joel, Amos, Obadiah, Jonah, Micah, Nahum, Habakkuk, Zephaniah, Haggai, Zechariah, and Malachi. These twelve books are sometimes called *the Minor Prophets,* not because they are of lesser importance than the others, but because the books are short. In fact, the Jews thought of the writings of these twelve prophets as one book.

The foundation of our house of the Bible, remember, was laid in the seventh century B.C. when the book of Deuteronomy was discovered in the Temple. It took approximately two hundred years for the books of Genesis, Exodus, Leviticus, and Numbers to be added to the foundation, and to come to be accepted as scripture by the Jews. And even though they had been reading the books of prophecy for a long time, recognizing their religious value, it took nearly two hundred more years before the Jews thought of the Prophets as scriptural text.

Sometime around 200 B.C., or maybe a little earlier, the section of the Old Testament the Jews called the Prophets was recognized as belonging with the Law as holy scripture.

So, in a period of roughly four hundred years, the Jews had put in the foundation of the Old Testament (and, therefore, the foundation of the Bible), and had the walls in place.

But what about a roof?

The Writings — a Roof for the Old Testament

If you asked, say, a hundred people who have some familiarity with the Old Testament which part they like best, most of them would answer, "the Psalms." Many modern Christians can repeat the Twenty-Third Psalm from memory. Passages from other Psalms are also familiar to us. We like them because they are splendid poetry, and because they deal with the low and high moments of the soul. They resonate with us as they focus on feelings of anguish, despair, hope, and the ecstasy of dwelling in the presence of God. They reside solidly in the life of the human spirit, which is the same from age to age.

The Psalms were very important to the religious life of the Jews. They were their hymns as well as their prayers. We suppose they were used in their public worship and as aids to their private devotions.

But the Psalms can't be attached to the Law, nor to the Prophets. They are a different kind of sacred literature.

In fact, there were several pieces of religious literature accumulated by the Jews and cherished by them, which belonged neither with the Law nor with the Prophets. To indulge in a little slang, we might call this group a mixed bag. Job has been described as a philosophical essay. Song of Songs is a poem about love. Lamentations is, well, a lamentation. Chronicles is a history of Jerusalem. Daniel is a story about some young heroes of the Jewish faith.

This section of the Old Testament also includes the books of Proverbs and Ecclesiastes, which contain various teachings about life and the human condition; and the stories of Ruth, Esther, Ezra, and Nehemiah. The Jews referred to this diverse group as *the Writings.*

The Writings Become Holy Scripture

There is evidence that not long after the Prophets began to be recognized as scripture, the Jews were already adding other books to their body of holy literature. It wasn't until some ninety years after the birth of Jesus that the Jewish family of faith finally decided which books they called the Writings were to be considered scripture. But by then, of course, they had been using them as scripture for a long time.

The Law was the foundation of the Old Testament. The Prophets form its walls. It is roofed over by the Writings.

And that's how the Old Testament was built.

Chapter Four

The Apocrypha —
Passageway from Old to New

Very few Protestant Christians today have ever seen the books of holy scripture called *the Apocrypha.* Most of these books are found in the Roman Catholic Old Testament, but are hardly ever included in Protestant versions of the Bible.

Then are the books of the Apocrypha holy scripture?

Well, yes and no.

The Old Testament, as we have it in Protestant Bibles, is the Hebrew Bible. It was written by the Jews in Palestine. It was written in the Hebrew language (except for a little bit — such as part of the book of Daniel — which was written in the Aramaic language, the language Jesus spoke).

But between the time the last of the Hebrew Bible was written and the time when the Christians began to formulate the New Testament, Jews living in Egypt collected a number of writings which they considered to be scripture. These Egyptian Jews were Greek speakers, so these "extra" books were either written in Greek or translated from Hebrew into Greek.

There are, as we count them today, fifteen books in the Apocrypha. They are: 1 Esdras, 2 Esdras, Tobit, Judith, the Additions to the Book of Esther, the Wisdom of Solomon, Ecclesiasticus, Baruch, the Letter of Jeremiah, the Prayer of Azariah and the Song of the Three Young Men, Susanna, Bel and the Dragon, the Prayer of Manasseh, 1 Maccabees, and 2 Maccabees.

The First Detective Stories

What's in these books?

Some of them are what we might call *moralistic stories* — that is, stories whose purpose is to teach us a lesson.

Tobit is said to be, perhaps, the first work of fiction in recorded literature.

The late Dorothy Sayers (creator of detective Lord Peter Wimsey) pointed out that the apocryphal books of Susanna and Bel and the Dragon are very early examples of the detective story. In each of these books, the prophet Daniel is the detective. He brings about Susanna's vindication by the strategy of separate interrogation of suspects. And he solves the case in Bel by relying on the evidence of footprints. Mystery writers have been using these principles in their stories ever since.

Like the book of Proverbs in the Old Testament, the Wisdom of Solomon as well as Ecclesiasticus belong to that class of writing known as *wisdom literature.*

The Prayer of Manasseh could be thought of as a book to read for public or private devotions. The Prayer of Azariah and the Song of the Three Young Men would remind most readers of the Psalms.

1 Esdras and 1 and 2 Maccabees are books of history.

2 Esdras is an *apocalyptic* book on the order of the Revelation of John in the New Testament (we'll be talking about apocalyptic literature when we get to the building of the New Testament).

The book of Esther in the Apocrypha is the same as the book of Esther in the Old Testament, except that it has been expanded so as to give it more of a religious character.

Are the Books Called Apocrypha Holy Scripture?

The Greek-speaking Jews in Egypt who produced these books thought so.

The apostles and evangelists of the early Christian church thought so. When the Old Testament was translated into the Greek language — a translation known as *the Septuagint* — the books of the Apocrypha were included. It was the Septuagint version of the Old Testament, rather than the Hebrew version, which became the holy scripture of the early Christian church.

But it wasn't long until some Christian leaders began to question the inclusion of the Apocrypha in the scriptures. "Shouldn't scripture be limited to books in the Hebrew Bible?" they asked. "These *extra* books are good reading and may be helpful to the spiritual lives of Christians. Christians should be encouraged to read them. But are they holy scripture?"

The great Bible scholar of the late fourth and early fifth century was named Jerome. The church fathers commissioned him to translate the Bible into Latin. When he did this, he decided that any books not in the Hebrew Bible could not be classified as holy scripture.

Jerome called these books found in the Greek Old Testament but not in the Hebrew Old Testament *apocryphal.* The word literally means *hidden* or *secret.* Today, though, it has taken on a different meaning in our language. When we say something is apocryphal, we usually mean it is dubious or not authentic.

Jerome put these books in his Latin Bible. But before

each one he included a note declaring that these books weren't really holy scripture. As time went by, though, scribes who copied Jerome's Bible grew careless about including these disclaimers. The books came to be seen as just books in the Old Testament, and people tended to accept them as part of holy scripture. Though scholars of the church continued to argue about whether the books in the Apocrypha were scripture or not, during the Middle Ages most Christians looked on them as scripture.

If that's the case, then why aren't these books in all our Bibles?

As we said, all Roman Catholic Old Testaments include the apocryphal books — with the exception of the Prayer of Manasseh and 1 and 2 Esdras. The Roman Catholic Council of Trent, held in 1546, officially sanctioned these books as holy scripture.

But Martin Luther, when he translated the Bible into the German language (a task he completed in 1534), grouped the apocryphal books in a separate section between the books of the Hebrew Old Testament and the New Testament. Originally, the King James Version of the Bible — the version many of us know best — followed Luther's example. If your church has an old pulpit Bible it probably has the Apocrypha between the Old and New Testament.

But because Luther treated the Apocrypha as *extra*

books, most Protestant Christians followed his lead by treating them as *not quite holy scripture.* As the years went by, Protestant versions of the Bible dropped these books — which is why, if you are a Protestant Christian, you have probably never read them.

The Significance of the Apocrypha

Then why should we bother with these Apocryphal books at all?

For a number of reasons. First of all, if we know something about the Apocrypha, we will have a better understanding of our culture. Writers from Shakespeare to Longfellow relied on its books for inspiration and subject matter (Shakespeare named his daughters Susanna and Judith, the two most notable women in the Apocrypha). One of our favorite hymns, "Now Thank We All Our God," is based on a passage in Martin Luther's translation of the book of Ecclesiasticus. Novelists, poets, and musicians have, over the years, found material for their work in the Apocrypha.

The Apocrypha has also played an important role in history. In the Apocryphal book 2 Esdras, the forty-second verse of the sixth chapter reads,

> On the third day thou didst command the waters to be
> gathered together in the seventh part of the earth; six
> parts thou didst dry up and keep so that some of them
> might be planted and cultivated and be of service be-
> fore thee.

Christopher Columbus read this and figured that if only
one-seventh of the earth is water, then it couldn't be
much of a trip from the west coast of Europe to the east
coast of Asia. In fact, he used this verse as part of his peti-
tion to King Ferdinand and Queen Isabella for the financing of his voyage. The Apocrypha, in other words, played
some part in Europeans' discovery of America.

It is also interesting material. Some of its books are of
a very high literary quality.

But the real reason we should know something about
the Apocrypha is that — if we think of the Bible as a
building — it is the passageway which connects the first
wing of the building, the Old Testament, with the newer
wing, the New Testament. It was written between the
writing of the Old Testament and that of the New Testament. So it is very helpful to us in understanding the nature of Jewish life and thought during the time of Jesus
and the early church.

The Apocrypha and Christianity

When Jesus was born, there were three main sects or branches of the Jewish religion — the Sadducees, the Pharisees, and the Essenes (more about them later). This intertestimental literature helps us see how they come into being, and the influence they had on the Christian story.

The Apocrypha shows us how belief in angels and demons — a belief prominent in New Testament times — came to have a place in Jewish religion.

The apocalyptic idea that God would soon bring the age to an end and establish a kingdom of righteousness through the Messiah was not peculiar to the Apocrypha, but is very prominent there. The Apocrypha shows us that the expectation of a Messiah was very much in the minds of the Jews when Jesus came preaching about the Kingdom of God.

The Christian doctrines of the resurrection of the body and of original sin — which we meet in the New Testament — have strong roots in the Apocrypha. None of the writers of the New Testament quote directly from the Apocrypha, but Paul and others make allusions which appear to be to the Apocrypha. It is safe to say that many, if not most, of the New Testament writers knew and were influenced by the Apocrypha.

Finally, returning to our metaphor, if you have a house with two separate wings, you need a passageway for getting from one wing to the other. You might be able to get from one to another without a connecting chamber, but it is convenient and helpful to have that passageway.

So, if we think of the Apocrypha as a passage which links the Old Testament to the New Testament, we will understand why — whether these books are holy scripture as some say, or are extra books as others claim — the Apocrypha is an important part of the structure of the Bible.

Chapter Five

The New Wing —
the New Testament

The first Christians saw no need to build onto the scriptures they already had — the Hebrew Bible which most Christians call the Old Testament. This was the Bible of Jesus. He not only referred to "the Law and the Prophets," he also frequently quoted from them.

Remember, too, that in the chapter on the Apocrypha we noted that these books show us the religious mood of the Jews when Jesus was born. It was a mood of expectation — expectation of God's Messiah coming soon to establish his righteous kingdom.

Jesus believed in this coming kingdom. After his death and resurrection, his followers were convinced that he was the promised Messiah, and that he would return soon to establish God's kingdom.

It's helpful to remember that the first followers of Jesus perceived themselves as Jews. They revered the Jewish scriptures. And, since they expected Jesus to return in their lifetime, they saw no need for a special *Christian* scripture.

The Q Document

Bible scholars believe that somewhere along the line someone — maybe many people — wrote down lists of things that Jesus had said and taught. Perhaps some of these lists were made by people who had actually heard Jesus speak. Others may have written down what they had heard from friends about what Jesus had said and done. It is possible that each Christian congregation had its own sketchy record of the words and deeds of Jesus.

All of this, we must note, is speculation. No such document (or documents) has ever been found. Nevertheless, most scholars are convinced that it once existed. They call it *the Q Document.* *Q* is an abbreviation of the German word *Quelle,* which means *source.*

Most scholars of the Bible believe that this vanished record, along with the Gospel of Mark, is the source material for the Gospels of Matthew and Luke. Perhaps even for the Gospel of John, though the writer of that book may have had Matthew and Luke in his possession, as well as some other source material.

The Q Document and the Gospel of Mark, then, would be the framework upon which the Christians built the New Testament.

Mark — a Movie Scenario

Mark is the oldest Christian gospel. It was written, most experts think, about A.D. 70. By this time, two generations of Christians who had never known Jesus had grown to maturity. We would guess that the leaders of the young religious movement, by this time known as *Christian,* reasoned something like this:

"It seems we have been wrong about God's timetable for the return of Jesus and the establishment of God's kingdom. Our children are growing up with little more than word-of-mouth knowledge of Jesus. Wouldn't it be wise for us to write down a permanent and authoritative account of Jesus' life and teaching?"

Mark is very brief. The style is blunt and powerful, with a strong emphasis on action verbs. It sounds like a scenario for a movie because something is always happening.

Matthew's Gospel and Luke's Gospel

The Gospel According to Matthew came out probably about ten years after the publication of Mark. Matthew relied heavily on Mark as a source for his book. Almost all of the Gospel of Mark is included in Matthew. It is, though, a longer book than Mark. Matthew must have had available to him sources of information about Jesus which Mark either didn't have or chose to ignore.

Then, about ten years after the publication of Matthew, the Gospel According to Luke appeared. Luke also relied heavily on Mark, including well over half of Mark's Gospel in his book. But Luke also included in his book material not found in either Mark or Matthew.

Today we call these three books *the Synoptic Gospels* — meaning that they cover much of the same material and they tell the same story. But this does not mean that they are alike in style or point of view.

As we have noted, Mark, is brief, almost sketchy, and powerful.

Matthew has been called the most Jewish of the Gospels. Matthew is quite anxious to convince the Jews that Jesus is the Messiah promised by the Old Testament.

Luke, on the other hand, was a Gentile, probably a Greek. He is not as interested as is Matthew in showing that Jesus is the Messiah to the Jews. He portrays Jesus as the savior for all peoples.

So each of the Synoptic Gospels — though they tell essentially the same story — has its own slant on these events. Each has a point of view to contribute. These three Gospels, then, became the first special Christian religious literature. At this stage in the history of the Christian church these three books — though widely circulated among Christians — were not yet looked upon as holy scripture. A Christian New Testament was still several miles down the road of Christian history. But the writing of the Gospels of Matthew, Mark, and Luke was the first step toward a distinct Christian holy scripture.

A Different Kind of Gospel

But aren't there four Gospels?

Yes. Around A.D. 100 to 110, as far as most scholars can tell, the Gospel According to John appeared. But John, while it also tells the story of Jesus, is very different from the three Synoptic Gospels.

By the beginning of the second century after Jesus, the church was fast losing its identification with the Jewish faith. Most new converts were coming from the Greek and Roman worlds. Quite naturally, they had little interest in a religion which was rooted in terms of Jewish faith and the Jewish expectation of a Messiah.

Some scholars think John's Gospel was commissioned by leaders of the early church; others believe it to have been the author's own idea. We do not know. We do know that the leaders of the church welcomed it gladly as a story of Jesus which would appeal to the Gentile mind. Yet they wanted it to be popular and accepted by all Christians. So they combined the Gospel of John with the three Synoptic Gospels.

Prior to the appearance of John's Gospel, Matthew, Mark, and Luke had circulated as separate books. They were already popular among Christians and widely accepted. The church leaders hoped this popularity would rub off on the Gospel According to John. And it did.

Whenever we try to sum up differences so complex as those between the Synoptic Gospels and the Gospel of John, we are likely to oversimplify. But we can say that John is more *doctrinal* or *philosophical* or *theological* than the other three Gospels.

A doctrine is a belief or an idea that someone or some group holds to be true. The Greeks loved to speculate about their beliefs and ideas relative to the nature of life and the world. The author of the Gospel of John knew how to talk their language.

He knew, for instance, that stories of Jesus' birth —

such as we have in Matthew and Luke — would not inter-est the Greeks very much. So he begins his story not with a genealogy or with the events leading up to a stable in Bethlehem or with adoring shepherds and angel choirs. Instead, he starts on a philosophical note by saying that Jesus is the living embodiment of God's eternal creative principle.

Most Jews wouldn't have cared particularly for this idea. They didn't think that way. But the Greeks thought that way. And that's why the Gospel of John, sometimes called *the Fourth Gospel,* was written.

The word *gospel* means *good news.* We think of the four Gospels as four versions of the life of Jesus. But they were written not just to tell Jesus' story, but also to con-vince people that Jesus was (and is) God with us. The story is told to carry a message, and that message is the good news about Jesus.

Is One of the Gospels Best?

Probably the Christians who first had the opportunity to read the four Gospels had their favorites. So do Chris-tians today. There was a tradition that Mark was a tran-scription from the lips of the Apostle Peter, and many early Christians would have liked it for that reason. Many

modern Christians appreciate its brevity and straightfor-
wardness.

Others opt for Matthew. It has been said that if we
could keep only one Gospel, it should be the Gospel of
Matthew because it tells us the most about the life of Jesus.

Still others like the Gospel of Luke the best. Luke, according to tradition, was a medical doctor. At any rate, he
shows great interest in and compassion for the sick. He
tells us about the Jesus who helps and heals. We like that.
And Luke, without question, was the finest writer of all
the Evangelists. Luke had the soul of a poet. The nativity
story, as he tells it, is one of the most beautiful pieces of
literature ever written.

We already noted that John would have appealed to
Christians with a Greek mind-set. Today it continues to
be a favorite of those of a theological bent.

Although, as we shall see, the letters of Paul were
written before the books of Matthew, Mark, Luke, and
John, it was these four Gospels which first attained the
status of holy scripture.

A Christian named Justin wrote a description of
Christian worship services he attended in Rome sometime around A.D. 150. He reported that the leader of the
service sometimes read from the Old Testament (which
was not called the Old Testament in those days, but

rather *the prophetic word*). Sometimes, though, Justin said, the worship leader read from *the memoirs of the Apostles,* which was what the early Christians called the books we know as the Gospels.

So, by the middle of the second century after Jesus, these four Gospels were apparently considered just as holy and just as inspired as the Old Testament — in Rome at least. And if these books were considered scripture in Rome, then probably most other Christian congregations looked on them as holy scripture as well. For Rome was the leading church of Christendom.

Why Were These Four Books
Perceived as Holy Scripture?

No one, so far as we know, had said that Matthew, Mark, Luke, and John were to be used as holy scripture. That came later. But they had been widely circulated among Christians for many years. They were respected for their usefulness as aids in and instructions for the practice of the Christian faith. They established themselves because of their merit.

Later, when they were accepted as appropriate works for use in Christian worship, respect for the Gospels was elevated to reverence. So these four books were treated as scripture before they were actually called scripture — or in other words, though no official Christian council had pronounced them to be equal in holiness to the Old Testament, they were treated as equal by their use in Christian worship.

So, in much the same way that Deuteronomy was the foundation on which the Old Testament was laid, the four Gospels became the first building blocks of the New Testament.

What about the Book of Acts?

In our New Testament, the Acts of the Apostles comes after the Gospel of John. It really belongs after the Gospel of Luke, because it is the companion volume to that book, the second volume of Luke's history of the rise of Christianity. It was published later than his Gospel, but was immediately recognized as a Christian book of immeasurable value. It is mostly about the lives of the apostles Peter and Paul. It did much to make Paul popular with the early Christians.

We can't quite think of it as a gospel, but it is a part of the foundation of the New Testament.

The Letters of Paul —
the Walls of the New Testament

If the four Gospels are the foundation of the New Testament, then the letters of Paul are its walls. The letters attributed to Paul, the great apostle to the Gentiles, make up the second-largest block of New Testament writings attributed to a single author. Only Luke's two volumes — his Gospel and the book of Acts — exceed the letters of Paul to the seven churches in bulk.

Interestingly, the walls of the New Testament were built before the foundation was laid. Paul, as near as we can calculate from the fragmentary information we have of his life, was probably executed by the Romans before the Gospel of Mark, the earliest Gospel, was written. His letters, then, were written, more than likely, before Mark sat down to write his gospel.

Then why aren't Paul's letters the foundation of the New Testament? Because they weren't collected and circulated until after the four Gospels were widely known and read by Christians.

Did Paul Intend His Letters
to Be Treated as Holy Scripture?

No.

Then why are they the walls of our New Testament?

To understand this, we need to know something about Paul. Like Jesus, Paul was raised in the Jewish faith. But unlike Jesus — who broadened and humanized the teachings of his religion — Paul, before his conversion, interpreted Judaic Law in its narrowest and strictest sense.

But on a trip to Damascus, the purpose of which was to persecute Christians, Paul had a sudden and remarkable change of heart. You can read about it in the ninth chapter of the Book of Acts. This happened, as best we can determine, two or three years after Jesus was crucified. So far as we know — though their lives overlapped — Paul never saw Jesus or met him in the flesh.

After his conversion to Christianity, Paul felt that God was calling him to preach this new gospel. So he spent the rest of his life traveling all over what we now call the Greco-Roman world, preaching and teaching and founding Christian churches.

But when a quarrel or a controversy broke out in one of the churches he had founded, Paul couldn't jump on the next jet and fly in to settle the problem the way a modern executive might do. The best he could do was write a letter.

So his letters, then, are mostly written to specific churches to solve problems which had arisen. They are the work of Paul the administrator who, through these letters, is striving to strengthen these young Christian communities.

Part of his job, as Paul saw it, was to help Christians in the various churches under his supervision to understand the Christian faith. Many of them had recently come to Christianity from other religions and had only a superficial knowledge of their new faith. This explains why Paul's letters are a mixture of practical counsel on how to handle problems in the church, judgments on how Christians should behave, and passages dealing with theological questions such as the motive and mission of Jesus Christ.

Scholars believe that most, if not all, of Paul's letters were written between A.D. 50 and 62.

How Many Letters Did Paul Write?

Probably a lot more than we have in the New Testament. We'd have to guess he wrote letters to other churches which somehow got lost. But today we have ten letters to

seven churches as the early Christian church reckoned it.
They are:

The Letter to the Ephesians

The Letter to the Romans

The First and Second Letters to the Corinthians

The Letter to the Galatians

The Letter to the Philippians

The Letter to the Colossians

The First and Second Letters to the Thessalonians

The Letter to Philemon

The Letter to Philemon was addressed to an individual, a wealthy Christian friend of Paul's. But the letter
makes it plain that Paul intended it to be read to the congregation of which Philemon was a member — probably
in the city of Laodicea. Philemon, then, was thought of as
a *Letter to the Laodiceans.*

There are other letters in our New Testament which
are attributed to Paul, but they are not addressed to
churches. We'll get to them shortly.

How Did Paul's Letters to the Churches
Become a Collection?

We can only speculate. But we do have some evidence to go on.

Our best evidence indicates that the book of Acts was widely circulated among Christians around A.D. 90. Acts tells us all about Paul's life as a traveling missionary for Christianity. These tales of Paul's journeys, his adventures, his hairbreadth escapes, his hardships and suffering as he sought to spread the Christian faith must have been exciting reading for the early Christians!

Many of them would have known little or nothing about Paul. But when the book of Acts was published, they wanted to know more about him. Then, when they discovered that he had died a martyr for the faith, those Christians would have recognized that here, indeed, was a Christian hero!

It has been pointed out that the Book of Acts could guide a person interested in collecting Paul's letters to seven of them. If some early Christian had the Letter to the Colossians and the Letter to Philemon, then the Book of Acts would tell him or her where to find the remaining letters to the churches.

So, the reasoning goes, some Christian at Colossae or Laodicea, who would have known about Colossians and

Philemon and possibly Ephesians (which most scholars think was meant to be read by the whole church and not just in Ephesus), set out to track down the other letters and, having done so, assembled them into a collection like we have today.

Detectives need corroborating evidence for their theories, of course. This particular one is strengthened by the fact that though Luke was not acquainted with the collection of Paul's letters, the author of the Revelation of John (writing not long after Acts was published) was very familiar with them. He addresses his book to "the seven churches that are in Asia." This choice of seven churches can hardly have been a coincidence.

Were Paul's Letters to the Churches Recognized as Holy Scripture When They Were Published?

No, not yet. Not for a long time, really.

Though they must have been widely read in the churches and highly esteemed by Christians, these letters of Paul were not considered to be holy scripture.

But about A.D. 140, a wealthy Greek Christian layperson named Marcion promoted the idea that the Christian Church should sever all connections with the Jewish religion. That meant discarding the Old Testament as the Bible of the church. Marcion said the Christian Church should have its own Christian holy scripture. In his opinion, this scripture should consist of the Gospel of Luke and the ten letters of Paul.

Though he had considerable support for a period of time among the churches, the church fathers ultimately said no, this wouldn't do. In the first place, they pointed out that the Christian faith was grounded in the Jewish religion. The Jewish scriptures were too precious to Christians to throw them out.

In the second place, Matthew, Mark, and John were too much a part of Christian life and worship to abandon them, they declared. So they pronounced Marcion a heretic, and his movement eventually subsided.

But his idea of a Christian scripture, or a New Testament, planted the idea in the mind of the church. And his high regard for the letters of Paul undoubtedly caused the early church to take them more seriously as literature appropriate not only for the education of believers, but for use in Christian worship.

And so, in short, a heretic was responsible for the idea of a New Testament.

A Variety of Writings Form the Roof
of the New Testament

The four Gospels, plus the book of Acts, we said, made up the foundation of the New Testament. The ten letters of Paul to the churches are its walls. But we need a roof, and that roof is composed of the twelve books in our New Testament which are left after we subtract the Gospels, Acts, and Paul's letters.

All of these books are written in the form of letters, but they have very little else in common. We'll discuss them briefly.

In addition to the ten letters of Paul to the seven churches, there are four other books in our New Testament traditionally attributed to Paul. They are:

The Letters to Timothy and Titus

Three little books — two letters to Timothy and one to Titus — are called *the pastoral letters.* Instead of being directed to churches, they are written to two of Paul's coworkers who were under his supervision. They are called *pastoral* because they offer the kind of advice we would expect a Christian pastor to give to those working with him in the church.

No New Testament scholars, whether of the conservative disposition or otherwise, believe that these letters as we now have them come from Paul's pen. Bible scholars trying to assign authorship of books follow a procedure very much like that of a detective analyzing evidence. They ask questions like the following:

- *Does the writing style of this book conform to the style of the books we know for certain this author wrote?*
- *Are the ideas expressed in this book consistent with the ideas in the books we know for certain this author wrote?*
- *Is there anything in this book attributed to this author which would confirm that it was written at a time during which the purported author was actually writing?*

With respect to the books of 1 and 2 Timothy, as well as Titus, the answer to all of these questions is No.

All writers have a style which becomes rather easily recognizable. They favor certain words and phrases. They follow certain patterns of syntax. Today, scholars can even run writings from long ago through computer programs to see whether they do in fact match up with their purported author's style.

1 and 2 Timothy aren't really much like Paul's known writings. Nor are the ideas expressed in these books basi-

cally similar to the ideas expressed in Paul's known works.

Perhaps more conclusive for most of us, the books reflect a period in Christian history somewhat later than Paul's lifetime. Briefly, they speak of bishops and elders as leaders of the church. This kind of church organization was unknown in Paul's day.

We don't mean to say that these aren't good books, splendid books, inspired books. The fact that Paul didn't write them — at least in their present form — in no sense detracts from their worth.

Nor does it mean that someone tried to cheat by claiming that Paul wrote them when he actually hadn't. Literary practice in New Testament times found it quite acceptable and entirely honest to put someone else's name on a book you had written.

The scholar-detectives say that they find bits and pieces of writing in these pastoral epistles which pass the test of having been written by Paul himself. They guess, then, that Paul was likely in the habit of sending brief notes of instruction to his several assistants — of whom Timothy and Titus were two. Then later, some Christian teachers or teacher who lived after Paul came across these notes and wanted to give them wide circulation. This would require editing and expansion, which would account for differences in style, thought, and/or historical setting.

In any event, no matter how exactly they came to us, the pastoral epistles make up a part of the roof of the New Testament.

The Letter to the Hebrews

No one knows who wrote the Letter to the Hebrews. It is not attributed to Paul, and it is very different from Paul's letters in style, ideas, and historical setting. The ideas in Hebrews reflect a kind of Christian thinking popular toward the turn of the first century — long after Paul's life had come to a close.

Early Christian scholars liked to guess who was the author of the Letter to the Hebrews. Some thought it had been written by Barnabas, Paul's colleague. Others suggested Luke, the gospel writer. Not a few said it sounded like the work of Clement of Rome, a prolific Christian writer who did his work near the end of the first century. Another early Christian scholar, Origen by name, said of the book, "The author is known to God alone." So far, Origen is right.

No matter its author, Hebrews is well written. Its purpose is, apparently, to inspire a renewal of faith among third-generation Christians whose zeal may have been flagging. Parts of it, especially the eleventh chapter, which is a great discourse on faith, are high on many modern Christians' list of favorite New Testament passages.

The Catholic Letters and the Letters of John

For purposes of convenience, biblical scholars group five New Testament books under the name *catholic letters.* That's *catholic* with a small *c,* meaning not Roman Catholic, but *general* or *universal* letters. They call them this because they aren't addressed to any particular church or person, but to all Christians.

The catholic letters are James, Jude, 1 and 2 Peter, and 1 John. They give advice about living the Christian life, discuss what is sound Christian thought and what is not, and warn against heresy. In short, they cover a multitude of subjects.

There are two other letters ascribed to John which earned a place in the New Testament. They are shorter than 1 John, personal notes really, offering us tiny glimpses into some of the issues an early church faced.

The Revelation of John

In addition to the Gospel of John and the three letters of John, the last book in the New Testament, the Book of Revelation, is attributed to John the disciple of Jesus. Revelation is written in the form of a letter too, but it really isn't one.

Revelation is a category of one in the New Testament so far as the type of literature it represents. It is what scholars call *apocalyptic* literature, meaning that its theme is the end of the age when God's ultimate purpose shall be revealed. It is full of symbols that are very strange to us but would have given comfort to early Christians who were suffering persecution by the Roman government.

With the addition of the pastoral epistles, the Letter to the Hebrews, the catholic epistles, the letters of John, and the Revelation of John, we have 27 books in the New Testament. Our building is now complete, although the Christian Church didn't decide as much until many, many years later. We'll talk about that next.

Chapter Six

The Canon: or, Who Said, *This Is the Official Bible?*

When Bible scholars use the word *canon,* they mean an authentic or recognized list. Our word *canon* comes from the Greek word for *reed.* The reed was used as an instrument for measurement. So when we speak of books being part of the canon of the Old or New Testament, we mean books which have measured up, so to speak, as authentic holy scripture.

But who decided which books measured up and which books didn't? Who said, "The house is finished. No more rooms will be added to it, now or ever"?

We should remember that not all the literature about or pertaining to a religion is looked upon as holy scripture. Only part of it is recognized as having been *set aside* in a special class. It carries sufficient authenticity and significance all its own to be regarded as holy scripture.

But how does a piece of writing become holy scripture? A traditional answer is, "God selected it." Even so, we still want to know about the process of selection. Fortunately, we have this history available to us. Many people and much debate played a part in the selection of the books which make up the Bible.

All sacred literature begins as oral tradition. People possess it in the form of stories and beliefs passed from one generation to the next by word of mouth.

The next step comes when someone says, "We ought to write all this down." Once the process of writing it down begins, though, it produces so much literature that at some point, people begin to pass judgment on all this religious writing.

Over a period of time, the followers of a faith reach a consensus on which writings are the most useful and precious to them. The main thing to keep in mind is that it takes a long time to do this. We'll describe briefly the long, slow process of deciding which books were ultimately included in the Bible.

The Old Testament Canon

We've already summarized the construction of The Old Testament. But even in Jesus' time, there was no official stamp of approval on the books of the Old Testament.

The Sadducees accepted only the Law (the first five books of the Old Testament) as scripture. Jesus refers to "the Law and the Prophets," apparently accepting them as holy scripture, as did many other Jews of his day.

But as late as the latter part of the second century after Jesus we find the Christian Bishop Melito of Sardis complaining that he really didn't know exactly what Old Testament books should be accepted as holy scripture, or in what order they should be placed.

The Council of Jamnia

Bishop Melito could have referred to the list of Old Testament books determined to be authentic scripture by a council of Jewish rabbis. We now refer to it as the Council of Jamnia, because Jamnia was the town where a rabbinical school was located and where the council met.

This event occurred approximately ninety years after the birth of Jesus. As we have seen, the Jews in Egypt accepted more books as authentic scripture than did the Jews in Palestine. These rabbis at Jamnia said, in effect, "We've got to decide once and for all which books are scripture and which aren't, or people will keep adding new books forever." Their decision was to limit the Jewish scriptures to the books in the Hebrew Bible — the books as we have them in most Protestant Bibles today.

But Bishop Melito probably didn't even know about this list. As we have noted already, the Bible of the early church was the Septuagint, the version of the Old Testament which had been translated into Greek, and which included the books of the Apocrypha — in short, the Old Testament favored by the Jews in Egypt.

So which version is holy scripture, and which one isn't?

Apparently — after much deliberation — the Jews settled on what we call the *Hebrew Canon* (the Old Testament as authenticated at Jamnia, and as we have it in today's Protestant Bible). This decision occurred sometime between 150 and 200 years after the birth of Jesus. Some scholars believe that, since by this time Christian literature (such as the Gospels or Paul's letters) was in wide circulation among Jews, it became necessary for Jewish leaders to say precisely what was and what wasn't holy scripture for Jews. At any rate, there wasn't much disagreement among Jews about what books to accept as scripture after this period.

The Christian Old Testament

But the argument among Christians continued. It went on, in fact, for hundreds of years. Though there were a number of books in dispute (the book of Esther, for example), the fundamental question was, "Should the books of the Apocrypha, which the Greek-speaking Jews considered scripture but the Palestinian Jews didn't, be scripture for the Christians?"

In our chapter on the Apocrypha we described how Jerome, when making his official Latin translation of the Bible, put qualifying notes before the books of the Apocrypha to indicate that they weren't quite in the class of holy scripture.

Then, more than a thousand years after Jerome translated the Bible into Latin, Martin Luther translated it into German. In setting aside the books of the Apocrypha in a separate section between the Old and New Testaments, and treating them as not quite measuring up to the standards of holy scripture, he determined a policy which Protestant Christians have followed pretty much since then. After all, he started the Protestant Reformation, so what he said carried a lot of weight.

Thus, Protestant Christians accept the Hebrew version of the Old Testament as holy scripture.

But not Roman Catholic Christians.

Because the Protestant Reformation posed a challenge to the Roman Catholic Church, it called a church council to see what it could do to meet the challenge. This famous conclave is known in history as the *Council of Trent*. It took place in 1546. And among the steps it took was to put an official Roman Catholic stamp of approval on the Old Testament, including therein twelve books of the Apocrypha.

That's why today Roman Catholic Christians have an Old Testament which is larger than the Protestant Old Testament.

However, though official councils and assemblies ended up pronouncing what is to be accepted as Old Testament scripture, the important part of the process is the testing of these books in the lives of faithful people. Over a period of time, they are the ones who decide what writings are especially valuable, helpful, and inspiring.

Some people might want to think of this as a human evaluation. Others will want to see it as a description of how God creates holy scripture. But either way, this is the history of how religious writings came to be set aside as especially authoritative for the followers of the faith the writings delineate. This is how the process works.

The New Testament Canon

We have already seen how the New Testament was built. We have pointed out that by A.D. 150, the Christian Church in Rome, at least, was using the Gospels of Matthew, Mark, Luke, and John in their worship services, even as they used the Old Testament scriptures. We have also seen that the Greek layperson Marcion wanted to form a Christian holy scripture out of the Gospel of Luke and ten of Paul's letters — and that the church rejected his idea. But we are still a long way from a collection of Christian writings recognized as authoritative for Christians. We are still several hundred years from a New Testament.

The opening stages in "the history of the New Testament Canon," or the process of deciding which books belonged in the New Testament, followed rather rapidly after Marcion planted the idea of a Christian scripture. But it took a long time for the church to "close the canon."

About the same time as Marcion, another respected Christian leader named Theophilus of Antioch praised the four Gospels and the ten letters of Paul. He doesn't say they are scripture, and he thinks a bit more highly of the Gospels than he does of Paul's letters, but in his comments we can see that the idea of a Christian scripture is obviously progressing.

Heretics Help Form the New Testament

The next stage in the development of the New Testament seems to have been brought about by a number of offbeat Christian doctrines being promoted through various writings. When you have all sorts of ideas, many of them conflicting with one another, claiming to be authentic Christian doctrine, people become confused. "Hold on," they say, "what is and what isn't true Christian doctrine?"

Once that question is asked, an authoritative collection, a New Testament, is inevitable. We could say, then, that a heretic (Marcion) planted the idea of a New Testament, and heretics made it necessary to form a New Testament. So heretics do have their uses.

The First New Testaments

Around A.D. 200 we begin to get lists of the Christian writings that various individuals believe are to be regarded as holy scripture. They all include the four Gospels and the ten letters of Paul. But these lists didn't always agree with respect to what other books belong in the New Testament.

For example:

A great Christian scholar named Irenaeus, who lived

and worked in Lyons, France, published a list of books which he determined to be Christian scripture. He said 1 Peter and 1 John should be in the New Testament (though he probably meant 1 John to include all three letters of John). He said the Revelation of John is Christian scripture. He also included a book called *the Shepherd of Hermas.* This was about A.D. 190.

A little later on, another famous Christian scholar, Tertullian of Carthage, published his list, and it included the Letter of Jude as well as the Shepherd of Hermas. Later on, though, he said he had been wrong to give the Shepherd of Hermas a place in the New Testament, that it was really not worthy of that honor.

There is a document, written by an unknown author about A.D. 200, called the *Muratorian Fragment.* It is, apparently, a list of Christian books regarded as holy scripture by Christians in Rome. It is pretty much like these other lists, except that it has two books of Revelation — the Revelation of John and the Revelation of Peter. The author does point out, however, that some Christian leaders have a low opinion of the Revelation of Peter and won't permit it to be read in their churches.

These lists can be thought of as the first New Testaments, although the New Testament as we have it today contains some books these lists don't, and discards some books that they include. But, so far as the history of the development of the New Testament is concerned, as soon as you have Christian scholars and leaders drawing up lists of Christian writings which are to be *set aside* as singularly authoritative, you have the beginnings of a Christian holy scripture.

Origen's New Testament

Anyone who reads the history of early Christianity will come across the name Origen. Origen lived in Alexandria in Egypt most of his life. He was born in A.D. 185 and died in 254. He was one of the truly great scholars of the early church.

Origen approached the task of deciding which books belonged in the New Testament and which ones didn't as any careful scholar would. He did extensive research, and then reported what he had discovered.

What he discovered was that certain books were accepted as scripture by nearly all Christians, while certain books were accepted by some Christians but rejected by others.

So Origen drew up two lists of New Testament books. The first list was made up of what he called the *accepted* books. On this list were the four Gospels; fourteen letters attributed to Paul (the ten letters to the churches, plus

1 and 2 Timothy and Titus, plus Hebrews, which many early Christians thought was written by Paul); the Acts of the Apostles; 1 Peter; 1 John; and the Revelation of John.

The second list he called the *disputed books,* and while he accepted them as holy scripture, he admitted that many Christians did not. This list included James; 2 and 3 John; Jude; 2 Peter; the Shepherd of Hermas, and the Letter of Barnabas. All these disputed books eventually became accepted books except for the Shepherd of Hermas and Barnabas.

The oldest complete manuscript of a New Testament that has been discovered up to now is called *The Sinaitic Manuscript.* The books found in this manuscript are exactly the books you get if you combine Origen's accepted list with his disputed list.

The architecture of the New Testament as we have it today, though, was far from settled in Origen's day. The idea that there should be a Christian holy scripture to go along with the Old Testament had been accepted by all Christians, but what should go in it had not.

The New Testament of Eusebius

A very important date in Christian history is A.D. 325. That is when the Roman Emperor Constantine (who may or may not have been a Christian himself, but favored Christianity as the religion for the Empire) convened the Council of Nicaea. This council was concerned with Christian doctrine rather than what was or was not official scripture.

One of the delegates to the council was Bishop Eusebius of Caesarea. Eusebius was well acquainted with activities occurring throughout the Christian world. He'd talked to leaders from all parts of it during the Council of Nicaea. He then wrote a *Church History* in 326, which has become one of Christendom's most famous documents. Eusebius makes no effort to conceal the fact that, as of A.D. 326, there was still wide disagreement among Christians as to just what Christian writings properly belonged in the New Testament.

Eusebius, though, had ideas of his own about what books should be included in a New Testament. While freely admitting that some of these books were not accepted by all Christians, he drew up a list of books which duplicates exactly the New Testament as we have it today. He does say, though, that he isn't entirely certain about the status that should be accorded the Revelation of John.

Athanasius

Another celebrated name in Christian history is Athanasius, Bishop of Alexandria. His strong-minded disposition got him in hot water with his Christian colleagues from time to time. Every now and then church officials would banish him, so he'd have to live in exile for awhile. This might have been inconvenient for Athanasius, but he lived in a lot of places (including France). Because of the frequency of his relocations, he was well acquainted firsthand with what Christians here and there and everywhere thought about the New Testament.

Athanasius always came back from exile, usually to new honors and positions of greater leadership in the church. As Bishop of Alexandria, he sent out a letter every Easter to the churches under his care. In A.D. 367 his Easter letter declared that some Christian writings should be read as holy scripture in worship services, while others were good reading and helpful to converts in understanding the faith, but weren't to be classed as scripture.

Athanasius recommended several books from the Apocrypha and certain other Christian writings as "good reading." But for Christian scripture, he lists precisely the same books we have in our New Testament today.

A great deal more discussion and disagreement with

respect to what was (or was not) Christian scripture occurred, but we've shown you how the process worked.

Jerome

In A.D. 382, Jerome began his project of making an official Latin translation of the Bible. This, as we have mentioned, is the Vulgate, the great Bible of the Middle Ages, and still the official Bible of the Roman Catholic Church. Jerome, who did extensive research before he translated the Bible, decided on a New Testament which corresponds to the New Testament in Bishop Athanasius' Easter letter.

So by the end of the fourth century after Jesus, the New Testament, Christendom's Holy Scripture, had achieved its final form. Debates continued, of course, but the general consensus among Christians was that the 27 books we have in the New Testament today are the ones that really belong there.

Gutenberg Closes the Canon

Actually, the issue was finally decided with the invention of printing. Johannes Gutenberg printed the first Bible about 1456, and it was the Vulgate version with our 27

books in the New Testament. After that, no one was in-
clined to argue about which books belonged in the New
Testament.

Chapter Seven

Decorating the House —
Translating the Bible into English

As we have noted, the Old Testament was written in the Hebrew language (except for a few snatches of Aramaic, the language spoken by Jesus). The Apocrypha was written in the Greek language, though some of its books were first written in Hebrew before being translated into Greek; and the New Testament was written in Greek.

But if you speak English, a Bible written in Hebrew and Greek isn't going to do you much good. You need it in the language with which you are familiar. So it needs to be translated into the language you can read.

Since we are thinking of the creation of the Bible as an analogy to home construction, it is appropriate to consider translating the Bible as decorating the house. And, just as the interior of a house becomes dated and needs to be freshened up from time to time by new paint and paper and drapes, so the language of the Bible, even translated into our tongue, has to be freshened up every now and then. The house has to be redecorated in order to make it a home.

Wyclif's Bible

Here's an example of why the Bible has to be translated and retranslated:

Nyl yee deme, that ye be not demede, for in what dome yee demen, yee schulen be demede.

These are the first and second verses of the seventh chapter of the Gospel According to Matthew. But the words are all but unintelligible to us, as John Wyclif translated this passage for the first English version of the Bible. This was in 1382. In other words, he was a contemporary of Geoffrey Chaucer. Those of you who have assumed the task of reading Chaucer's *Canterbury Tales* in Middle English have encountered the same frustrating language barrier.

In the King James version of the New Testament, these same verses read,

Judge not, that ye be not judged. For with what judgment ye judge, ye shall be judged; and with what measure ye mete, it shall be measured to you again.

John Wyclif, like most pioneers, was ahead of his time. It was more than a hundred years after Wyclif brought out his English Bible that anyone else showed real interest in getting the scriptures out of Hebrew, Greek, and Latin into languages people read and spoke. For hundreds of years, no one except scholars who could read one or more of these languages could read the Bible at all.

A Dutch scholar by the name of Erasmus, a contemporary of Martin Luther, was apparently the first voice of authority to lobby for the idea of translating the Bible into the languages of the people. Erasmus held no position in the church, but he was popular, his writings were widely read, and he had strong opinions which he wasn't shy about expressing.

In 1516, Erasmus published the first printed Greek New Testament. He took the occasion to say he thought that all people should have a Bible they could read. "I would wish all women, girls even, to read the Gospels and the Letters of Paul," he wrote, which was a shockingly progressive idea for his era.

Martin Luther took him seriously. Although the Latin version of the Bible had been translated into German, Luther wanted to prepare a German translation which really spoke the language of ordinary people. It is said that he haunted the butcher shops and marketplace in order to be familiar with the way the common people used language. At any rate, his translation of the Bible — which he based not on Latin versions but on the original Hebrew and Greek manuscripts — is credited with creating the modern German language.

Opposition to English Translations

Today, all churches encourage and even plead with their members to read the Bible, so it isn't easy for us to imagine the opposition within the Christian church itself to the early translation of the Bible. These were the days when the Protestant Reformation was flowering, and change was in the air. Since many of the translators were individuals who held reformist views, the established church tended to resist their work.

William Tyndale

William Tyndale was an English Christian who believed the only way a person could really know God was through the holy scriptures. But there was no modern printed English Bible. Wyclif's Bible wasn't printed until much later, and anyway, its language was out of date by the sixteenth century. So Tyndale set out to translate the Bible into the kind of English, he said, that even a plowboy could read and understand.

Tyndale read Greek, so he translated the New Testament first. Because of opposition to his work by church leaders in his own country, he moved to Germany so he could have his English New Testament printed there. This was in 1525.

When Tyndale's New Testament was circulated in England, it achieved a strong popularity. But the established church did its best to destroy all copies, and pretty well succeeded, because only one copy of Tyndale's New Testament survives today.

Tyndale was persistent, though. He learned the Hebrew language in order to translate the Old Testament, and he did manage to complete and publish the Pentateuch. But in 1535, opponents of his work managed to have him arrested (in Belgium), and a year or so later he was executed. But this did not halt the movement to translate the Bible into the language of the people.

The Coverdale Bible

Myles Coverdale published the first complete printed English Bible in 1535. Interestingly, no one knows who printed it or where. It was most likely printed, like Tyndale's incomplete Bible, somewhere on the European continent.

A friend of William Tyndale, John Rogers, had possession of Tyndale's translation, including part of the Old Testament that Tyndale hadn't been able to publish. He added to it his own revision of Coverdale's translation of the remainder of the Old Testament. The Rogers Bible became the first English translation licensed by the King for publication and sale in England.

An English revision of the Bible made by Richard Taverner was published in 1539. That same year, the famous *Great Bible* made its appearance. It was a huge book, designed to be placed on a lectern or reading desk in churches for use in public worship. But people were also encouraged to come in and read it whenever they wished. So that no one would steal it, it was secured to the lectern by a heavy chain. It was, therefore, nicknamed the Chained Bible.

The Invention of Bible Verses

Most of us think of the Bible as made up of numbered chapters and verses. We know, for example, that John 3:16 is the 16th verse of the third chapter of the Gospel according to John. More people, probably, can recite that partic-

ular verse by heart than any other passage in the Bible —
with the possible exception of Genesis 1:1. We tend to assume that the Bible always existed with those divisions
into chapters and verses.

But it didn't.

The chapter separations as we have them today date
from the twelfth century. And the chapters themselves
were divided into numbered verses by a French printer
named Robert Étienne. Étienne was interested in the
convenience of the printer rather than the edification of
the reader. Thus his verses sometimes break off in the
middle of a thought or sentence or paragraph.

People think of Bible verses as complete units in
themselves, but they seldom are. Versification may help
us memorize Bible passages, but it can have a down side
as well, often interfering with the understanding of what
a verse is saying by taking it out of its context. Étienne's
New Testament with numbered chapters and verses was
published in 1551.

Nicknaming Bibles

We can tell how popular the various translations were
with the people because nearly all of them were known by
nicknames. We've mentioned the Chained Bible. The

Geneva Bible, which was translated by English Puritans living in Geneva, Switzerland, was called the Breeches Bible because it translates Genesis 3:7 thus: "and they sewed fig leaves together and made themselves breeches."

The Geneva revision was followed by a revision of the Great Bible, officially known as the Bishops' Bible, because so many bishops had a hand in the project. The people, though, often referred to it as the Treacle Bible because it translates Jeremiah 8:22 as "Is there not treacle in Gilead?"

Myles Coverdale's Bible had, by this time, been nicknamed the Bugs Bible because it translates Psalm 91:5, "Thou shalt not nede to be afraid of any bugges by night." The first printing of the King James version misprinted Ruth 3:15 to read, "and *he* went into the city." It became known as the He Bible. The next printing made the appropriate correction, changing the pronoun to *she*. Of course, this version was predictably nicknamed the She Bible.

The King James Translation

The translation of the Bible which has dominated the English-speaking world for nearly four centuries now is the King James version published in 1611. Yet it came into being almost by accident.

On Monday, January 6, 1604, King James I of England was in residence at Hampton Court, some miles from London, because London was beset by the plague. English Christianity had been divorced from Rome by King Henry VIII. But the Church of England, when James came to the throne, was split between the High Churchmen and the Puritans.

It was to see if this rift could be patched up that James had called representatives of both factions to meet with him. The relations between the factions were as chilly as the weather; they spent most of the day arguing.

At some point in the discussion, though, Dr. John Rainolds, a Puritan, president of Corpus Christi College in Oxford, and reputed to be the most learned man in England, said to the King, "May your majesty be pleased to direct that the Bible be now translated, such versions as are extant not answering to the original."

At this time, the Bishops' Bible (or Treacle Bible) was the authorized version. But the Geneva (or Breeches) Bible was probably the most popular among the English-speaking people. The Bishop of London, a High Churchman, opposed Rainold's suggestion, as did others.

King James, however, fancied himself a student of the Bible. He had once revised a few of the psalms, and had written a commentary on the book of Revelation. And he didn't care for the Geneva Bible: "I profess I could never yet see a Bible well-translated into English, but I think that of Geneva is the worst."

The upshot of this meeting was that, though the High Churchmen and the Puritans didn't reconcile their differences, they did get together on the project of translating the Bible.

Fifty-four scholars were selected to carry out the project, which, officially, was to revise the Bishops' Bible. Some of them died during the six years it took to complete the translation and were replaced. They were divided into three groups. One group met at Westminster, one at Oxford, and one at Cambridge.

We might assume that King James, having commissioned the translation, would have paid for it. But he didn't. However, as King, he had the right to award a *living* — that is, a Church of England parish — to anyone whom he chose. So those scholars among the fifty-four who needed jobs received a living from the King. Some of them, in fact, became bishops.

Interestingly, only one of these scholars' names is widely known today. Lancelot Andrewes, Dean of Westminster, became and remains famous not so much for his help in translating the King James version, but for a devotional book, now considered a classic — *The Prayers of Lancelot Andrewes.*

Experts today give much credit to Dr. Miles Smith, editor of the project, for the superb quality of English found in the King James version. We need to remember that this is Elizabethan English, the language of Shakespeare and *The Book of Common Prayer.* It is English at its best.

Yet the King James Bible was not immediately accepted. It was a publishing success, as new translations nearly always are. But people complained that the language wasn't elegant enough, or that it wasn't as orthodox as it should be, or that it didn't conform strictly enough to the original manuscripts. It just wasn't as good as the versions they were used to, the people said.

Nevertheless, after more than three centuries the King James Bible still stands as a superb work of art — perhaps the only significant work of art ever produced by a committee. The rhythms and cadences of the language hang in our memory. The sheer loveliness of so many passages makes them unforgettable.

The late H. L. Mencken was a militant atheist, but an acknowledged authority on the English language. Mencken said of the King James Bible, "It is probably the most beautiful piece of writing in all the literature of the world."

Other English Translations

The Roman Catholic English translation of the Bible, known as the Douay Bible because it was completed at the Catholic English College at Douay, France, was published in 1610 (the New Testament had been translated and published in 1582).

Once begun, translating and revising the Bible became the thing to do, apparently, among scholars and religious leaders. New discoveries of ancient manuscripts of the Bible, or part of the Bible, encouraged a proliferation of new translations and revisions.

For 250 years, however, the new translations were private efforts rather than projects commissioned by the Church of England. They are too numerous to mention individually. But one example would be John Wesley's translation of the New Testament.

Wesley, the founder of Methodism, published in 1755 the manuscript he called *The New Testament With Notes, for Plain, Unlettered Men Who Know Only Their Mother Tongue.* Wesley had a passion for bringing education to the common people, so his stated purpose for translating the New Testament is characteristic of his ministry.

For the most part, it is safe to say that most of the translators had the same purpose as the motive for their efforts. They wanted a Bible that ordinary people could read and understand.

Around 1870, British experts began a revision of the King James Bible. A number of Greek and Hebrew manuscripts had surfaced since the original King James version had been published. This put scholars in a more advantageous position to ensure that the English corresponded closely to the original Greek and Hebrew meanings. This Bible, published in 1885, is known as the Revised Version. American scholars didn't agree entirely with their British counterparts with respect to some of the wording in the Revised Version, so they made some changes in it and published it as the American Standard Version in 1901.

The Revised Standard Version, a mid-twentieth-century revision of the American Standard Version, was prepared by the same process which produced the King James Bible. A group of American scholars was selected and commissioned (by the International Council of Religious Education as well as the National Council of Churches) to revise the American Standard Version, which was of course a revision of the King James version.

Like the King James version, it has been a publishing success coupled with criticism. The criticisms of the Revised Standard Version of the Bible sound similar to the objections expressed against the King James Bible when it was first published.

Hebrew Poetry and Common Greek

Two discoveries — one about the Hebrew language in which the Old Testament was written, and another about the Greek language in which the New Testament was written — have made it possible for modern revisers and translators of the Bible to make it more meaningful and understandable to English readers.

A professor of poetry at Oxford University said, around the middle of the eighteenth century, that he thought some of the Old Testament — notably parts of the prophetic books — were not prose, but poetry. It took a long time for revisers and translators to take this idea seriously. But all the newer revisions print the poetic passages as poetry.

Then, shortly before the end of the nineteenth century, a German clergyman named Adolf Deissmann was looking at some examples of recently discovered Greek papyri dating from New Testament times. The papyri consisted of the kind of paper generated by everyday life, such as personal letters, bills, legal documents, and the like. He saw that the Greek used in these papers was not like the classical literary Greek with which he was familiar.

It was, though, very much like the language in his Greek New Testament. Up to this time, it had been assumed that the New Testament had been written in literary Greek, because no one knew — though some observers had guessed — that there was a common, everyday version of the Greek language. But with the discovery of all the non-literary Greek papyri, students and experts now had a basis for a new and expanded understanding of the language in which the New Testament was written.

Recent Revisions and Paraphrases

We could say that translating, revising, and paraphrasing the Bible — like decorating and redecorating a house — is a process that never ends.

The Revised Standard Version, which we met earlier in this chapter, was itself revised to produce the New Revised Standard Version in 1989. This Bible updates the language of its predecessor. For example, God is not referred to with the old-fashioned pronouns "thee" and "thou," but with the more familiar "you."

In recent years many new versions of the Bible have made their appearance.

The New English Bible (translated under the auspices of the Church of Scotland, the Church of England, and such "free" churches in Britain as the Methodists, Presbyterians, Quakers, and Baptists) has been highly regarded since its publication in 1970. Unlike the Revised Standard Version, the New English Bible is an entirely new translation rather than a revision of an earlier English Bible.

Another recent translation of the Bible is the New International Version. This version was prepared by scholars holding conservative theological viewpoints who wanted a modern version which would be more attractive to evangelical Christians than the Revised Standard Version.

Yet this is just the beginning. The Confraternity Bible; the Phillips New Testament; the Knox Bible; the Scofield New Testament; the Berkeley Version; the New Testament in Plain English; the Amplified Bible; the New World Translation; the Good News Bible; the Jerusalem Bible; the New American Bible — these are names of some, but by no means all, recently published versions of the holy scriptures.

Paraphrases of the Bible have also become very popular. A paraphrase does not translate the original Greek and Hebrew word for word, but instead attempts to broadly convey the message of the Bible in the colloquial

English we speak today. Two very well-known paraphrases of the Bible are *The Living Bible,* the work of a
conservative evangelical Christian named Kenneth Tay-
lor; and *The Message,* produced by Eugene Peterson, a respected pastor and theologian.

Are All These Revisions Necessary?

Yes.

Our house may be well constructed, but to make it a
good place to live the rooms must be decorated so that
the people who live there find the house comfortable as
well as attractive. This means that, every now and then,
the house needs some redecorating. Language is like our
taste; it changes with time. What one generation finds
pleasant and meaningful the next generation may find
dated and unappealing.

The idea behind the decoration and redecoration of a
house is to enhance the building's best architectural
qualities — to emphasize the true value of the house.

So it is with the revision of the holy scriptures.

The building is there. It is well and solidly constructed. What the translators and revisers are trying to
do is to reveal to us what was in the minds of the builders,
because they seek to tell us what was in the mind of God.

The house will always be there, but the decoration will change from time to time. This is the only way to keep the Bible fresh, alive, appealing, and relevant to succeeding generations.

Biblical Terms You Need to Know

When you listen to people discussing the Bible, terms such as *Pauline* or *Aramaic* or *redactor* are likely to pepper the conversation. It can be helpful and informative to know what these terms, as well as others, mean. This is a *short* short list. For anyone who wants to make a thorough study of biblical terminology, a good Bible dictionary is essential.

Apocalyptic Literature Religious writing predicting the end of the age, at which time God would establish a righteous kingdom. The Revelation of John, the last book of the New Testament, is an example of apocalyptic literature.

Apocrypha The fifteen books included in the Old Testament used by the Jews in Egypt, but not in the Old Testament used by the Jews in Palestine. Twelve of the books in the Apocrypha are still regarded as holy scripture by Roman Catholic Christians, but not by Protestant Christians.

Aramaic   The language Jesus spoke.

Canon   The list of books in the Old and New Testaments which are accepted as holy scripture.

Catholic Epistles   The five letters in the New Testament not addressed to a specific person or individual church, but rather to all Christians. The catholic (meaning *general*) epistles are 1 John, 1 and 2 Peter, James, and Jude.

Dead Sea Scrolls   These scrolls were part of the library of a community of a Jewish sect called the Essenes which had been located near the north end of the Dead Sea. The community was destroyed by the Romans in 68 B.C. No doubt anticipating the destruction, the Essenes hid these scrolls, sealed in jars, in nearby caves. They were discovered in 1947. Some of the scrolls are copies of the Old Testament (except for the Book of Esther), including a splendid scroll of Isaiah. Some are commentaries on various Old Testament books. Some have to do with patterns of living in the Essene community, while others contain prayers and other materials intended for group worship.

Essenes   One of the three major divisions or sects of Judaism at the time of Jesus' birth. They lived in a community of their own.

Evangelist   One who brings good news. Matthew, Mark, Luke, and John are, by church tradition, called *the four evangelists.*

Gospel   A word meaning, literally, *good news.* The first four books of the New Testament are called Gospels.

Hexateuch   The first six books of the New Testament. While the first five books of the New Testament have been looked on since around 400 B.C. as a unit of scripture, Bible scholars often consider the first six books, the Hexateuch, to be a single literary development.

Israel   Sometimes used to designate the entire Jewish nation or religion. More specifically, when the Jewish nation broke up into northern and southern kingdoms (926 B.C.), the northern kingdom was called Israel.

Law   (also *Pentateuch* or *Torah*) Designates the first five books of the Old Testament. They form the first section of the Old Testament. The Law is one of the three types of literature into which the Hebrews divided the Old Testament. Some Jews, including the Samaritans and the Sadducees, recognized only the Law as scripture.

Johannine Literature   The Books in the New Testament which carry the name of John as author and are traditionally attributed to John, the disciple of Jesus: the Gospel According to John; the three Letters of John; and the Revelation of John.

Judah   The southern kingdom of the Hebrew nation.

Messiah   Hebrew term meaning *anointed one. Christos,* from which the name *Christ* is derived, is the Greek equivalent of *Messiah.*

Pastoral Epistles   The letters in the New Testament (attributed to Paul) which are addressed to Christian missionaries, and containing pastoral advice from their director or superior. The pastoral epistles are 1 and 2 Timothy, and Titus.

Pauline   Referring to the apostle Paul. *Pauline letter* or *Pauline doctrines,* for example.

Pentateuch   First five books of the Old Testament. Also called the Torah or the Law.

Pharisees   One of the three major divisions or sects in the Jewish religion at the time of Jesus' birth. Jesus himself was most likely raised in the tradition of the Pharisees.

Q Document   A written record (or possibly records) of the sayings of Jesus, and perhaps stories about him, which many scholars believe was the source material (along with the Gospel of Mark) for the Gospels of Matthew and Luke. No copy of a Q document has ever been discovered, however.

Redactor   One who puts literary material into suitable form, much like an editor. A good deal of the Old Testament was prepared by redactors, organizing and editing the Hebrew scriptures.

Sadducees   One of the three divisions or sects of the Jewish religion of Jesus' day. The Sadducees were the temple aristocracy of Judaism.

Septuagint   The Greek translation of the Old Testament. It was the scripture of the Jews living outside Palestine, mainly in Egypt. The early Christian church used the Septuagint as its Bible rather than the Hebrew version. The Septuagint, unlike the Hebrew Old Testament, contained the Apocrypha. Often abbreviated *LXX*.

Synoptic Gospels   Matthew, Mark, and Luke. Called *synoptic* because they cover substantially the same material in a narrative format.

Testament   A covenant or agreement.

Writings   One of the three classifications of literature in the Old Testament. The Writings are Old Testament books classified neither as Law nor as Prophets.

Appendix B

Some Dates That Will Help You
Understand How the Bible Was Built

We have seen that the building of the Bible took place over a very long span of time. The time line below will help you see just how long. Keep in mind that a great many of these dates are approximate.

1800 B.C.	Abraham migrates to Canaan and founds the Hebrew nation.
1500 B.C.	Hebrew people in captivity in Egypt.
1230 B.C.	Exodus from Egypt.
1200 B.C.	People of Israel, after forty years of wandering in the wilderness, arrive in the land of Canaan.
1000 B.C.	Saul becomes Israel's first king.
995-965 B.C.	Reign of King David.
965-926 B.C.	Reign of King Solomon. The Great Temple is built in Jerusalem.
926 B.C.	The nation of Israel becomes two separate

kingdoms — Israel in the north, and Judah in the south.

750 B.C.   Amos, the first of the great literary prophets, appears on the stage of Jewish history.

722 B.C.   Israel (Northern Kingdom) conquered and annexed by Assyria, disappearing from history.

621 B.C.   The book of Deuteronomy discovered in its Temple hiding place, whereupon King Josiah declares it the law of Judah.

586 B.C.   The Exile. Babylon conquers Jerusalem, destroys the Temple, and carries the people to Babylonia.

540 B.C.   Persians conquer Babylonia. Exile ends in 538, when Jews return to Jerusalem.

515 B.C.   Great Temple rebuilt.

A little after 400 B.C.   The Prophets and the Writings accepted as Hebrew scriptures alongside the Law.

300-198 B.C.   Egyptians rule the Hebrew people.

About 250 B.C.   The Old Testament is translated into Greek, and, later, supplemented with books not found in the Hebrew Old Testament.

198-168 B.C.   Syrians rule the Jewish people.

168-64 B.C.   Maccabean revolt gains period of Hebrew independence.

64 B.C.   Romans take over Palestine, so Hebrews are once again a people subject to a foreign power.

Sometime between 6 and 0 B.C.   Jesus is born.

Some Dates That Will Help You

Sometime between A.D. 27 and 33   The crucifixion of Jesus.

A.D. 50-62   Paul writes the letters (now part of the New Testament) to the churches.

A.D. 70   Gospel of Mark appears.

A.D. 80   Gospel of Matthew appears.

A.D. 90   Gospel of Luke appears (followed shortly by second volume of Luke's history, the Acts of the Apostles).

About A.D. 90   Jewish Council of Jamnia fixes Hebrew canon at the 39 books found in current Protestant Old Testament.

A.D. 100 to 110   Gospel of John appears.

First part of second century A.D.   Many Christian writings published, including books which eventually were accepted as part of the New Testament.

A.D. 140   Marcion urges the elimination of the Old Testament from Christian reading and worship. He proposes instead that the Gospel of Luke and the ten letters of Paul to the churches be the only Christian scripture. Eventually labeled a heretic and his doctrines discarded, Marcion nevertheless planted the idea of a Christian holy scripture.

A.D. 150   The four Gospels are in use as holy scripture by the church at Rome, and perhaps elsewhere.

A.D. 325   Council of Nicaea called by Roman Emperor Constantine to settle questions of Christian doctrine. Now accepted by the Roman government, the Christian church is no longer the target of persecution. Questions of doctrine are settled at this council, but there is still no offically accepted New Testament.

A.D. 367   Bishop Athanasius of Alexandria sends out Easter letter to his churches naming the Christian books which are to be considered as holy scripture. His list is exactly the same as the 27 books we have in the New Testament today.

Around A.D. 380-382   Jerome begins the authorized Latin translation of the Bible, known as the *Vulgate*. He includes the Apocrypha in the books of the Old Testament, but notes that they aren't to be considered canonical. He uses Bishop Athanasius' list of New Testament books for his translation.

A.D. 1382   John Wyclif publishes the first English translation of the Bible.

A.D. 1456   Johannes Gutenberg, the inventor of movable type, prints the famous Gutenberg Bible at Mainz, Germany. It is Jerome's Latin translation, the Vulgate.

A.D. 1522   Martin Luther brings out his German translation of the New Testament.

A.D. 1526   William Tyndale's New Testament printed. Printed in Germany, it is the first printed English version of any part of the Bible.

A.D. 1534   Martin Luther completes the translation of the Old Testament and Apocrypha into German. He puts the books of the Apocrypha between the Old and New Testaments. Eventually, these *intertestamental books* disappear from most Protestant Bibles.

A.D. 1535   Myles Coverdale publishes the first complete Bible to be printed in English.

A.D. 1546   The Council of Trent pronounces Jerome's Latin Bible, the Vulgate, the official holy scripture of the Roman Catholic Church. As a result, the Catholic and Protestant New Testaments are the same, but the Catholic Old Testament contains twelve books from the Apocrypha.

A.D. 1611   Publication of the King James Version of the Bible.